Beaded Earrings
Techniques & Designs

By
Rex & Ginger Reddick

Published by Crazy Crow Trading Post
P.O. Box 847 • Pottsboro, TX 75076
(903) 786-2287 • www.crazycrow.com

By
Rex and Ginger Reddick
Illustration & Design By
Dennis Graham
Photography By
Ginger Reddick & **Dennis Graham**

ISBN 1-929572-20-4

TABLE OF CONTENTS

INTRODUCTION

This book is designed for anyone interested in making beaded earrings, whether you're a beginner or advanced craftsperson. Now, other books on this subject have been published in the past, but none of these texts have featured detailed, full-color illustrations and photographs showing step-by-step instructions in a clear and straightforward manner. Such details are very important for anyone just learning to make beaded earrings. Our book provides complete instructional details, as well as patterns, graphs, and recommended materials and supplies. In addition, the easy-to-learn techniques herein can be carried over to making pendants and necklaces of your own design.

Our book progresses from basic how-to techniques and on to advanced instructions, many of which have not been previously published. In addition, there are lots of full-color graphics and numerous photo examples of completed earrings and pendants. These should inspire you with creative ideas for colors and design variations of your own.

The techniques described are based on experience gained by us through our many years of doing beadwork of all types, including making beaded earrings. We hope that these techniques will provide the reader with the skills for either beginning or advancing in this art form, as well as assisting in improving your speed and efficiency as that experience grows.

Today, with a renewed interest in beaded earrings and pendants, plus the demand for quality, handmade craftwork being at an all-time high, making and selling these items can pay off handsomely while requiring only a small initial investment. So, by studying the instructions and suggestions in this book, taking pride in your work, and using your imagination on colors and designs, you will undoubtedly discover an interesting and rewarding pastime.

The authors would like to thank Aileen Keylon, Sherrie Keylon, Cathy Griggs, Sharon Parker, Jessica Reddick Gatlin, and Issy Umscheid for their generosity in supplying some of the earrings shown in the photographs.

Beads are as old as mankind and the earliest forms were created using shells, stones, seeds, metals, bones and teeth that were pierced and strung into earrings, bracelets and necklaces for personal adornment. The bow drill is almost as old as civilization and was used extensively to drill semi-precious stones such as amethyst, lapis lazuli, agate, carnelian and garnet as long ago as three thousand years before Christ. These stones were ground and polished into beautiful and valuable beads that were traded extensively throughout the world.

Beads made of glass were first formed and wound in Mesopotamia and the Causcasus region of Russia as early as 2340 BC. Glass technology then spread to Egypt, Rome and the Middle East, eventually reaching its zenith in Venice, which became the primary center of bead and fine glass production for the entire world for several hundred years. By the year 1292, the glass factories were relocated to the island of Murano in order to protect the secrets of the glass making industry and to reduce the risk of fire to the city on the mainland. These secrets were so jealously guarded that for craftsmen who tried to leave Murano with this technology, the penalty was death!

The worldwide bead trade continues today, with the addition of other centers of production, including the Czech Republic, Japan and China. While the earliest beads were drilled, the perforation of glass beads is the result of their various methods of manufacture. Many types are produced today, including wound, drawn, pressed, spiral, folded and blown beads. These are much more efficient methods than drilling and have resulted in a vast array of relatively inexpensive beads that are in use by people scattered all around the globe. It is primarily with these glass beads that we are concerned, although other types may be incorporated in the creation of the earrings and necklaces discussed in the following pages and can lend a nice variety to the finished product.

10/0 = Approximately 130/Square Inch; 3120/Hank		12/0 = Approximately 228/Square Inch; 4560/Hank	
11/0 = Approximately 187/Square Inch; 4080/Hank		13/0 = Approximately 273/Square Inch; 5040/Hank	

Remember that beads are a unique and versatile medium for creating works of art, the only restriction being our own imagination.
When ordering beads, it is important to know that the higher the number, the smaller the bead. For example, a 12/0 bead is smaller than an 11/0 bead. The projects in this book generally call for size 11/0 seed beads and #3 or #5 bugles, but 12/0 beads can be used as well. Even smaller beads can be used with the projects that are made without bugles. Also, if you are just beginning, we recommend using size 11/0 seed beads with #5 bugle beads, since they are easier to work with than the smaller sizes and are well-suited when used together.

Bugle Beads

Bugle beads are glass tubes which are usually round. They are made in either straight or twisted styles and are commonly available in several different lengths ranging from 3/16" up to 1". Primarily, sizes #2, #3 and #5 are used in the projects described in this book,

Bugle Beads in Various Lengths

but other sizes can certainly be used. Shades of color will vary slightly with different dye lots and sizes can also vary slightly from batch to batch and from color to color. When purchasing #2 bugles, make sure this size will match well with any other beads you are using for your project. For example, if a #2 bugle bead is too small, you may wish to use a size #3.

Bugles can be used for the bottom portions or fringe of any of the projects that follow. Common sizes are 15, 20, 25 and 30mm, in this case with the size denoting their length in millimeters, NOT the diameter of the beads. A 25mm bugle is 1" in length. By shopping around, you may locate different types of bugles, such as twisted or octagonal cut bugles which create a nice effect due to the the way in which they reflect light.

When purchasing any type of bead, be sure to obtain enough to complete your project. If you happen to run out and have to buy more, the color may be the same number or name, but it could vary slightly if it comes from a different dye lot.

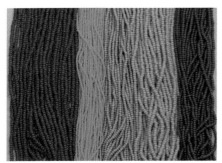

Opaque Seed Beads

Opaque Beads

Opaque seed beeds are the most commonly used beads in traditional American Indian beadwork. They are solid and light will not pass through them or reflect from them. When working with transparent beads, it is often helpful to use opaque beads along with them in order to provide contrast, which helps prevent blending of designs with the background and also helps make the lighter colors stand out better.

Transparent Beads

These beads are made of transparent, colored glass which allows light to pass through them, a characteristic that is especially useful in creating "fire" or "rainbow" effects. They are excellent for use in earrings and work well when used with all other types of beads such as cut beads and color-lined beads.

Cut Beads Showing Iris, Opaque and Transparent Colors

Cut Beads

More correctly known as "Charlotte" beads, these are seed beads that have tiny, randomly ground facets or "cuts" which reflect light and give them a unique sparkling effect. They are readily available in sizes 11/0 and 13/0 but can occasionally be found in sizes 15/0 and 16/0 as well.

Another type of cut bead that is widely available is the 3-Cut, which has an irridescent, luster finish. Normally found in size 12/0 in a wide range of colors, this size is well-suited for making earrings and the facets combined with the luster finish create a unique appearance.

Silver-Lined Seed Beads

Silver Lined Beads

These are transparent, colored beads which have a silver lining. The transparent glass allows light to pass through and reflect off of the silver lining. Silver-lined beads work great for highlights. If used effectively with opaque beads, silver-lined beads make very pretty jewelry and are a favorite type of bead for earrings and necklaces.

Color Lined Beads

Lined, or color-lined, beads have a colored center with an outer layer of either clear or transparent colored glass which give them a unique and very attractive appearance. However, they tend to blend together if not coordinated with contrasting colors within the design. They are also prone to lose their color if exposed to direct sunlight for long periods of time. An aurora borealis finish will give them a unique, multi-colored glimmer.

BEAD SIZES AND TYPES

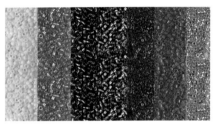

Delica Beads

These beads have a perfect, cylindrical shape and are extremely uniform in size and shape, making them an excellent choice for brickwork, gourd stitch and loomwork, as well as most styles of earrings.

Delica Beads

They are available in a wide variety of colors and have large holes that easily allow multiple passes of the thread which is quite advantageous when making beaded earrings.

BEADING SUPPLIES

Needles

Needles are like beads in that the larger the number, the smaller the size. It is common practice to use a size #11 needle with a size 11/0 bead, a size #12 needle with a size 12/0 bead and so forth. However, using a size smaller needle than the bead size you are using works better for most projects, so use a size #12 beading needle with size 11/0 beads. If working on a project that requires passing the needle through a bead many times, or working with silver-lined beads with a thick coating of silver, then drop down to an even smaller size needle, like a #13.

Thread

Thread is available in several different sizes, colors and types, but it is recommended to use white Nymo in size "A" or "B". Nymo is a strong, nylon thread that is excellent for beadwork of all types. Size "B" is a little heavier than size "A".

However, as with needles, when working on a project that requires that the thread must pass through a bead several times, size "A" thread would be preferable.

Beeswax

Beeswax is used to coat beading thread to strengthen and prolong the life of the thread. Thread coated with beeswax is also less likely to tangle or be cut by sharp bugle beads while working on projects.

Ear Wires

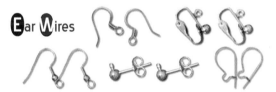

Although there are many different types of ear wires to choose from, the French style is the most popular style used. They are heavier than some of the other types of wires on the market and are more comfortable to wear. Other styles suitable for earrings include Fishhook Ear Wires and Kidney Ear Wires, as well as Ear Clips, for those whose ears are not pierced. "Stud" posts are also a popular choice, as are hoops.

Catches

Barrel, Magnetic, Lobster and Toggle Clasps are excellent for beaded necklaces and are available from most craft supply firms. They are made in silver or gold finishes and are inexpensive, efficient and easy to work with. You may also choose a sterling silver catch, but may pay a little more.

Graph **P**aper

Another handy item for making earrings is graph paper for planning your designs. Included at the end of this book are several pages which will allow you to color in your designs for use as guides when making earrings and necklaces. We recommend photocopying these blank designs so you can save the original pages for making future copies, as needed.

Tools & **B**ead **C**ontainers

There are a few other items that will be helpful when working with beads, such as plastic jars, containers or zip-lock bags, in which to store your beads, a small pair of sharp scissors such as those used for embroidery, a single-edge razor blade, sharp tweezers, and an awl. A clean, soft beading surface is best and a pressed pillow case folded twice or a piece of white buckskin works quite well for laying out small amounts of the different beads you will be working with. Other methods are the use of several small dishes or saucers, with each used to hold one bead color or type, or a partitioned paper plate with sections being used to keep the different beads separated.

Buying beads in hanks (beads temporarily strung on strings consisting of 10 to 12 loops of beads per hank), means they are usually more uniform in size than buying loose beads by the ounce. This is not always the case, but it is a general rule-of-thumb for you to remember. Some suppliers sell loose beads that are as high in quality as strung beads. For example, Delica beads are extremely high quality in both size and shape but are always sold loose. When buying supplies, shop around, ask questions and compare the products available.

As a guide for the first time buyer, a list of recommended supplies with which to begin making beaded earrings is included below. These items have been carefully chosen so as to allow you to complete several projects by using the same supplies and simply using different color combinations. Of course, you should feel free to select other colors or types of beads if you prefer, so choose those that are most pleasing to you and that you will enjoy working with.

- One hank each of Opaque 11/0 Seed Beads: Black, White, Red, Orange, Yellow, Turquoise, Royal Blue, Light Green and Pink.
- One hank each of Silver-lined 11/0 Seed Beads: Aqua Blue, Silver, Gold, Pink, Yellow, Red and Green
- Two or three ounces each of size #2 or #3 Bugle Beads: Black, White, Silver, Aqua and Pink.
- Two ounces of longer Bugle Beads in three colors for use in making dangles.
- Size "A" Nymo Thread, Size #12 Beading Needles, Beeswax and Earwires. Barrel Catches are needed if you intend to make jewelry with bead necklace chains.
- Graph paper is supplied in the back of this book, but it is a good idea to make photocopies and use them, saving the originals for future use. Color codes are included with the graphed projects, but the main colors have been left up to you to choose.

PRACTICAL SUGGESTIONS

Many mistakes may be made when first learning how to bead. The following things are most important in order to help you avoid some of these frustrating errors. If you do make mistakes, don't worry, as they can all be corrected! Everyone makes mistakes and it is all part of the learning process.

1) It is always best to work in natural sunlight. However, if you must work using artificial lighting, it is best to use a strong incandescent light bulb. Fluorescent lighting can be used; however, it tends to distort colors.

2) Thread is inexpensive. It's a lot easier to work with too much thread, which can later be cut off, rather than running short and trying to tie knots or work with thread that keeps slipping from the eye of the needle. You will soon learn the approximate amount of thread to use on each project, but until then, be free with the thread, using enough length so that you feel comfortable that you will have enough.

3) Always try to be aware of what you have just completed and know where you are going next. When building the tops of your piece, be careful that you don't skip any beads, always going straight up and down or side to side. If there are EVER any strings showing between beads, a bead has been left out and you will need to correct this immediately. Backtrack until you find the mistake then slowly work the thread out of the beads until you reach the mistake and then start beading again. It's much easier, faster and a great deal less frustrating to catch your mistakes as they occur and correct them at that point. Periodically sit back and look at your work from a short distance away.

14

This allows you to make any adjustments or corrections at that point rather than having to cut apart a finished piece of jewelry, thus wasting time and causing unnecessary frustration.

4) Color combinations and knowing how to use contrasting colors in any project is just as important as the technical aspect of beading. You may be able to produce the best made beadwork, but if the colors all blend together, the piece will not be attractive because the designs will be compromised. Black and white are universal colors and can be coordinated with almost any other color. Using these two colors can be very helpful as they are useful in separating similar colors to provide good contrast. The use of contrasting colors is a very important technique that makes the designs stand out from background colors and enhances the details in designs. For example, to break up light colors, use darker colors and to separate two dark colors, use white or a similarly light color.

5) Many of the different kinds of beads are quite beautiful and have unique characteristics, but by themselves they tend to lose their effectiveness when compared to being used in combination with appropriate other types. Begin by using the suggested combinations in the color charts or choose colors from some of the photos of completed earrings shown here. When you feel more comfortable working with the colors, then you can try using two or three basic combinations of opaque colors you have chosen yourself. You can also use black or white if necessary in order to separate the colors and make the designs stand out. In this way, you will achieve more satisfaction from your beginning efforts. Save experimenting for later down the road when you become more familiar with various combinations of colors and bead types.

BugleBeadBaseRow

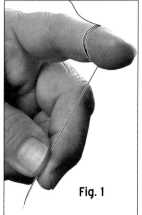

Fig. 1

The "base row" is the beginning of a project and can be made using either seed beads or bugle beads. For this first example we will use bugle beads and construct a project that is 7 beads wide.

Begin by threading your needle with about 2 yards of waxed thread. Wrap the end of the thread around your left index finger 5 or 6 times. Begin wrapping at the top of your finger and wrap away from you so that the thread ends between your index and middle fingers, coming toward you. See Figure 1.

Now select 14 bugle beads of the same size and color and set them aside. This is 7 beads for each earring and they can be either size #2 or #3. String the first 7 of these bugles on the thread and slide them all the way down until they are resting against your index finger. Pinch the thread with your thumb and middle finger, locking the bugles in between, as shown in Figure 2.

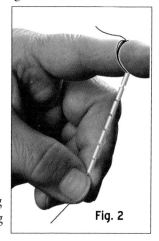

Fig. 2

Leave enough slack in the thread so that you can work the bugles together and move them up the thread. The slack will be slowly taken up as you sew them together. If you don't leave enough slack, the work will be too tight, and it will be difficult to move the beads along the thread as required. This can be frustrating and will be more time consuming as well.

Fig. 3

Starting with the second bugle above your thumb and middle finger, push the needle through this bead only and pull until the loop in the thread is tight (Figure 3). Grasp the bottom two bugles while maintaining light tension on the thread with your index finger and gently pull the thread until the bottom two bugles roll together. Again pinch the thread between your thumb and middle finger just below the bottom bugles (Figure 4) and repeat this procedure with the third bugle, then the fourth, and so on until you reach the last bugle.

Fig. 4

Keep the thread wrapped around your index finger, always maintaining light tension on it until the foundation row is completed. The tension will help the thread stay in place on your finger and also allow you to easily adjust the bugles along the string as you work your way to the end of the thread. It is best to keep the strung bugles facing to the inside of your hand as shown in Figure 5.

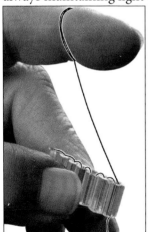

Fig. 5

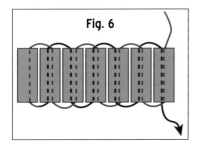

Fig. 6

After all 7 bugles in the foundation row are sewn together (Figure 6), they should be reinforced by making another pass of the thread through each bead. Simply run your needle back up through bugle #6, then down through bugle #5 and so on until reaching the first bugle on the opposite end. At this point the bugles should be sewn snugly together with the ends of the thread on opposite ends and opposite sides of the foundation row (Figure 7).

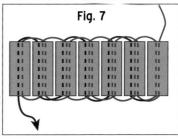

Fig. 7

Seed Bead Foundation

If you prefer to create a foundation using seed beads instead of bugles, simply follow the same steps as described above, replacing each bugle with a section of seed beads. These can be stacked 2, 3, or 4 high depending on your design layout. The trick to making seed bead foundations is to resist the temptation to apply too much tension on the thread during the beginning steps. Tighten the seed bead foundation on the second pass. Figure 8 shows how this type foundation is constructed.

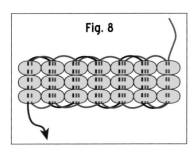

Fig. 8

TOP SECTION

This step will form the top portion of the earring or necklace and utilizes the "brick stitch" technique to taper the beads from the foundation row up to the apex of the work. One bead at a time is added here, beginning at one end of the foundation row.

If you are right handed, hold the beads in your left hand and if you are left handed hold the beads in your right hand. Hold the completed foundation row with the loose thread side up and away from you and working from the back, thread the needle through the top layer of thread that connects the first and second bugles together.
Make sure that you do not miss or only partially catch the thread connecting the bugles.

Pick up the first seed bead of this row and pass the needle under the thread between the first and second bugle as shown in Figure 9.
Pull the thread gently until the slack is almost out. If this thread is too tight, you can pass the needle be-tween the first two bugles and pull it up under the thread. The first bead should now rest at a slight angle on top of the bugles so you see the bottom of the hole. Keeping the needle above the thread that connects the two bugles, go back up through the bead you just at-tached and pull the thread snug to anchor this bead in place. It should now be centered over the top of the first two bugles of the foundation row as shown in Figure 10 .

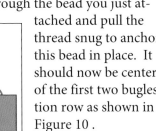

Fig. 10

Fig. 9

Pick up the second bead of this row and repeat this process, with this bead being centered over the second and third bead of the foundation row. Continue this sequence until you have reached the end of the foundation row.

The string should be coming out and up of the last bead you attached as shown in Figure 11. Run the thread down through the outside bugle, coming up through the second bugle, and then up through the last bead on the first row of seed beads. At this

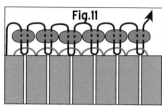

Fig.11

point all the beads should be fastened to the foundation row and both ends should be securely tied down. See Figure 12.

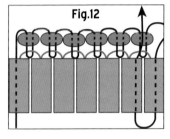

Fig.12

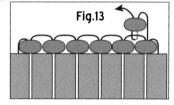

Fig.13

Start and finish all the following rows of beads in the same manner as described for the first row (Figure 13).

This process leaves an outer thread along both sides of your work. This produces a much nicer finished product when the ends on both sides are tied down neatly and uniformly rather than having one side tied down and the other side more loosely attached. When tying down only one side at the beginning of a row, the work often looks unbalanced. Add successive rows to the top section as shown in Figure 14 until you reach the top two beads, again tying the last, (second) bead down as before.

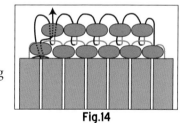

Fig.14

The Hanging Loop

To make the hanging loop for attachment to earwires, pick up four beads with your needle and sew down through the top of the pyramid, beginning with the bead that does not have the thread coming out of it (Figure 15). At this point you can either keep sewing

Fig.15

The Hanging Loop

down through the outer row of beads until you reach the foundation and go through the outer bugle as shown in Figure 16. Or, you can run your thread back up through the top six beads and complete a circle through all of these as in Figure 17. Then you run your needle through the outer beads as described above. This method is preferred due to the extra strength provided by the second pass of the thread.

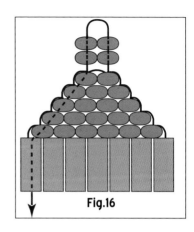

Fig.16

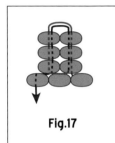

Fig.17

Fig.18

An attractive and quite simple variation to a typical earring is shown in the photo to the right.

After the top section is completed, the two outside bugle beads in the base section are sewn together, thus forming a "round" earring.

Fig.19

There are a number of ways to build the top portion of brick stitch style earrings and pendants using either bugle beads or seed beads for the foundation, but no matter what style top you decide to work with, they can all be used with any of the various style dangles described here. The most common style dangle is in the form of fringe, the part that hangs loosely from the stitched piece of your work. This style is universal and will work nicely with any of the tops you decide to use.

These dangles should swing freely, just touching the top portion of the beaded piece. If attached too tightly, they will not hang correctly. If they are not tight enough, they will sag unevenly with gaps between the top and the dangle. Although this is a simple step, it can be tricky, so be sure that you maintain an even tension on the thread and be sure it is pulled all the way through the dangles and not pinched between any of the beads, as they will loosen when the project is completed and leave a drooping dangle.

After completing several dangles and again when the piece of work is completed, go back and check your work. With the piece lying flat, gently roll the dangles back and forth with a little downward pressure. This helps work out any extra tension in the dangles and at the same time lets you check that the dangles are not too loose. It's also important to watch your count and sequence of beads as it is very easy to miss a bead or get a color out of place and not even notice the error until the piece is finished. Concentrate not only on what you are doing, but also on what you have done; and be consistent!

Always work on one side and in one direction when adding the dangles, as this leaves you with the thread showing only on one side.

If you are working on a design that is not symmetrical, such as a rose or other non-geometric design, we suggest working on one piece from right to left and then working from the other side of the second piece (from left to right). This allows you to work on both pieces from the front side in order to make sure that they match when finished.

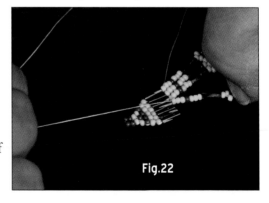

Fig.20

To add the first dangle of the fringe, lay the top of the piece flat on your working surface and pick up the beads required, sliding them all the way up the thread until they just touch the foundation row. Then separate the last four beads which will form the tip of the dangle, pulling them down and slightly away from the other beads as shown in Figure 20.

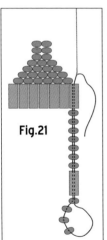

Fig.21

Run the needle back up through the bead that is just below the bottom bugle, continuing through the bottom bugle and up through the bugle in the foundation row (Figure 21).

If the dangles you are making are longer than your needle, you will have to complete the dangle in two steps. First, run the needle through as many beads as you can comfortably manage, and holding the three bottom beads with one hand, pull the slack out of the thread (Figure 22).

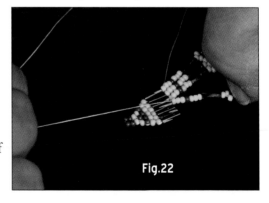

Fig.22

At this point you should feel the beads in the dangle hit the bottom of the foundation row.

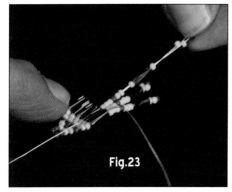

Fig.23

Next, run the needle up through the remaining beads and through the bugle or beads of the foundation.

Hold the last (tip) bead at the bottom of the dangle with the thumb and index finger of your left, and with the index finger of your right hand pressing down on the foundation row, use your thumb and middle finger of your right hand to pull the remaining slack out of the thread (Figure 23). The single bead at the bottom (tip) end of the dangle prevents the thread from being cut by a sharp bugle bead. Run the needle down through the next bugle or row of beads of the foundation and repeat the above steps until you have finished all of the dangles. Whenever possible, add or subtract 3 or 4 beads on each dangle in order to give a sharp, stair-stepped drop in the design. As a general rule, the beads will average out in size and give you the sharply defined lines necessary for quality bead work. Once in a while you will have to pull the beads off and adjust them to the necessary size in order to fit the pattern you are working on. Again, always check your work as you move along!

If the thread breaks or you run out of thread while working on the dangles, tie a knot inside the bottom bugle of one of the dangles. To do this, pull off the desired length of new thread, and with the new and old thread side by side, tie an overhand knot as shown in Figure 24.

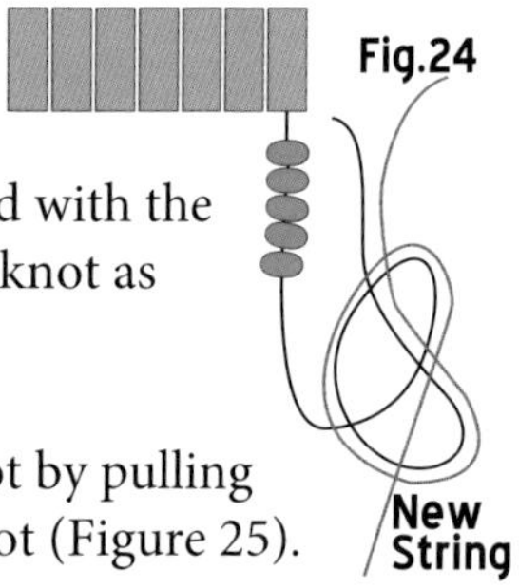

Fig.24

At this point you can adjust the length of the knot by pulling on one of the two strings on either side of the knot (Figure 25).

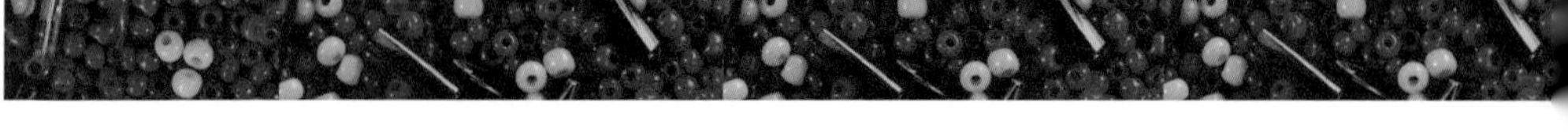

New String

Separate and pull the old string to shorten, or pull on
the new strings to give more length in the string where
the knot will be. When the knot is in the desired spot, tie the two
old strings in a simple square knot and cut off the excess string so
that it is short enough to stay inside the bugle (Figure 26).

Fig.25

When you have completed all the dangles, slowly roll
them back and forth while gently pulling downward
as described at the beginning of this section. The dangle should lie flat
without any crimps or gaps. Now examine your work from a short
distance, checking to make sure the bead count and colors are correct
in each dangle and that they hang evenly. Any mistakes should be
readily apparent at this point. If you notice an error, remove the needle and pull the thread out of each dangle by firmly pinching the tip
bead and pulling until the thread comes all the way out of the dangle.
Continue this until you reach the mistake, then
re-thread the needle and continue until the dangles
are finished.

Fig.26

When the dangles are finished, the thread needs to be
tied off. Run the needle back up into the top portion
of the piece and tie a knot between two of the seed
beads, pulling the thread tight. Next, run the needle
up through several other beads, pulling the knot up
into one of the beads if possible, or as close as possible so that it will be
less noticeable. Cut off the end of the thread by using the side of the
scissors rather than the points.

This will help avoid cutting any of the internal threads that hold the
piece together. Now thread the other end of the thread that is still
loose and run it up into the beads, knotting it and cutting it off as
explained above.

When making earrings and pendants, there are literally hundreds of different dangle variations possible by simply changing the beads, lengths, shapes, colors and/or designs. Changing only one or two of these components can change the overall appearance of the piece. All of these variations are fashioned using the same basic techniques as previously explained for making the pendant dangles, so we will rely primarily on illustrations and photographs to show how they are made.

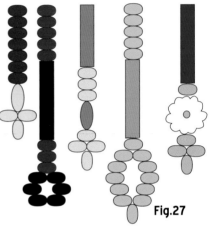

Fig.27

Quill Dangles

Fig.28

One interesting and simple variation when making dangles is to use porcupine quills that have been cut into tubes that resemble creamy white bugle beads. Quills range in length from approximately 1" to 3", and this allows you plenty of freedom in determining how long

you wish to make them. For an added design feature, they can also be trimmed with or without part of the brown tip remaining. See Figure 28.

Quills should be washed before use and ordinary dish soap works quite well for this. They should be rinsed well in warm water and then spread out to dry if they are not going to be processed immediately. While they are still damp they are soft and can be easily cut to length without cracking. If you plan to trim them later, they should be dampened first so as to avoid splitting or breaking them. As an added variation, porcupine quills are easily dyed using commercial *Rit*™dyes and following the directions on the package.

Once they are trimmed on both ends, a long heavy pin can be run through them to clear the pithy center, thus preparing them for stringing. Remember to keep the longest lengths slightly shorter than your longest needle so that they can be easily strung. Cutting a number of these at once and storing each length in a separate container or in a partitioned plastic box for future use will greatly speed up the beading process.

Depending on their length, quills can be substituted for bugle beads or a number of seed beads in a dangle. However, they are not substantial enough to be used for the base row.

Fig.29

DANGLE VARIATIONS

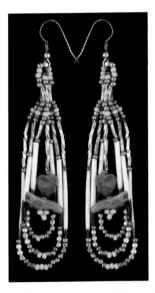

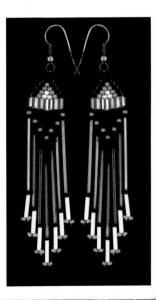

Loop Dangles

Fig.30

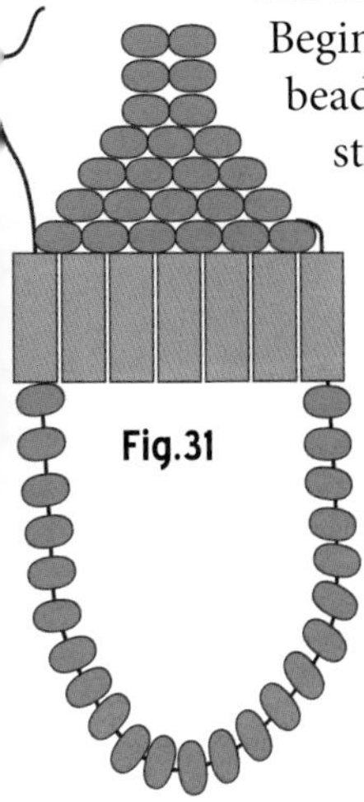

Another variation is the loop dangle and these are formed by making a series of loops, one inside the next as shown in Figure 30. Begin at the outside bugle (or row of beads) in the same way as making standard style dangles. Instead of ending the dangle and going back through the beads, string enough beads to make a full loop that reaches to the other side of the foundation row. Then run your needle up through the last bead on the opposite side, thus forming a loop (Figure 31). Adjust the tension on your thread so that each loop hangs nicely and is not too tight.

Fig.31

Next, come down through the second bead from the outside in the foundation row, adding beads to complete the loop. Run your needle up through the second bead from the outside on the opposite side of the foundation row. This is illustrated in Figure 32. Each loop is shorter than the previous one so that they hang inside one another as you proceed. Continue to add enough loops to complete the design and then tie off the thread as described for regular dangles.

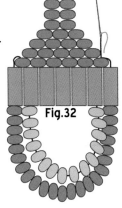

Fig.32

The Top Portion

A unique variation on the typical beaded earring is the style made using only bugle beads for the top rows as well as the foundation row. When the foundation row is completed, the next row is added in the same manner as you would when using seed beads, and tapering the earring by making each subsequent row one bead narrower. This forms a slimmer, more tapered earring with a unique shape. See Figure 33.

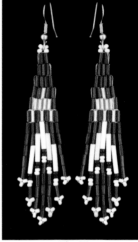

Fig.33

Fig.34

The top of the earring is finished in the same way as the conventional style and should also be made using an outer thread along both sides of the work, as previously described. This technique helps maintain a uniform shape to the earring as well as giving it a much neater finished appearance. Add successive rows to the top section until you reach the top two beads, as shown in Figure 34.

The Attachment Loop & Dangles

The attachment loop is made in the same manner as the regular earrings, using seed beads. The fringe on the bottom is made with either bugle beads or regular seed beads, matching or complimenting the top part of the earring. Seed beads and bugle beads can be mixed as shown in the above photo and other variations such as small glass fire-polished beads in size 4mm may be added if desired.

The brick stitch is uniquely suited to the production of beaded earrings as it forms a symmetrical piece of beadwork and is quite versatile. You may begin at the top and work down, or at the bottom and work up, depending on which is most comfortable for you. This may seem a bit confusing at first but it becomes much easier with a little practice.

Increasing the Brick Stitch

Most craft workers prefer to begin at the bottom with a foundation row of beads stacked at least 2 high (Figure 35). See Page 18 for the instructions on creating a seed bead foundation. To begin adding the next row, put 2 beads on the thread and slide the needle under the thread connecting the first and second beads of the foundation row

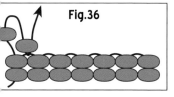

Fig.36

(Figure 36). This is done in the same manner as normal brick stitch; however, the first bead

Fig.35

will hang slightly over the foundation row as illustrated in Figure 37.

Continue as you normally would to build the brick stitch until you reach the end of the row. Select one bead on the thread

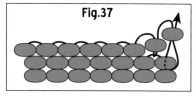

Fig.37

and run your needle down through the last bead on the foundation row. Then go back up through the bead you just added, as shown in Figure 37.

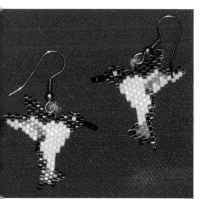

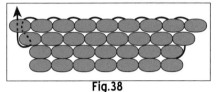

Fig.38

Pull the thread snugly and continue adding rows. Only one of the end beads on each row will have thread showing on the outside of the piece you are working on (Figure 38).

Continue following these steps until you have reached the center of your design, which is the longest row of beads in the pattern (Figure 39). Now begin decreasing each row as described earlier in the normal Brick Stitch instructions until you reach the top, 2-bead row

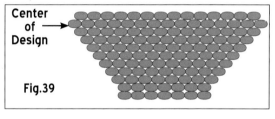

Center of → Design

Fig.39

(Figure 40). Now add 6 more beads to create the hanging loop as described in the section on Forming the Top. This will secure the top section and you can then run the thread all the way down the side beads until you reach and exit the foundation row (Figure 41).

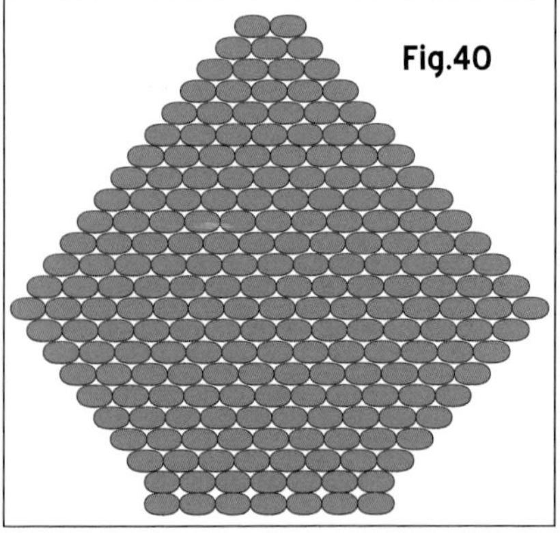

Fig.40

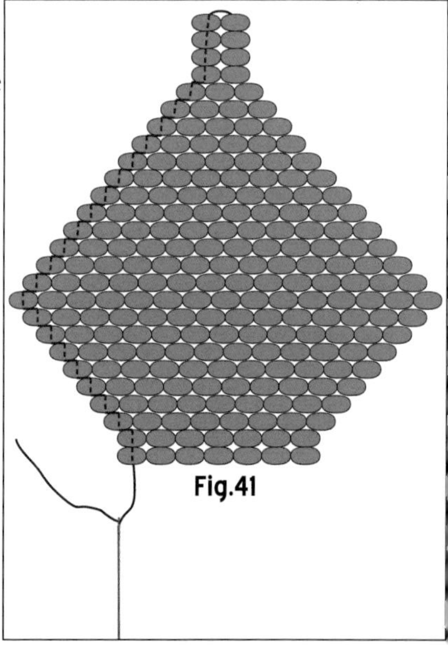

Fig.41

You are now ready to add the dangles of your choice.

Decreasing the Brick Stitch

Begin by creating a foundation row of your choice. Figure 43 shows a base row of 2 beads. Work your way up to the top of the project in

Fig.43

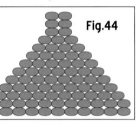

Fig.44

the normal manner, adding 4 beads at the top for the ear wire hoop (Figure 44). To decrease the bottom portion, simply turn the piece over (Figure 45) and begin adding the decreasing rows as previously explained. When you complete the last row, (Figure 46) turn the piece over again and add dangles of your choice. The number of beads in the last row will determine the number of dangles required, which is 7 in this example (Figure 47).

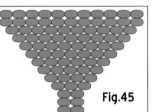

Fig.45

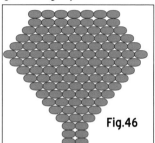

Fig.46

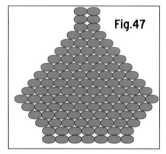

Fig.47

Fig.42

 **Double Stacking the Brick Stitch**

Fig.48

With this particular style of brick stitch, you can use a triple base row, 3 beads high (Figure 48). This is made in the same way as any other foundation row, except that 3 beads instead of 2 are used in place of each bugle bead.

Also, when this project is completed there will be no thread showing on the outside of any beads because none of the ends will be tied down as described in any of the previous Brick Stitch directions.

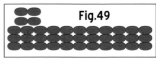
Fig.49

Begin the first row above the foundation row with 4 beads on your thread and slide the needle between the second and third beads of the foundation row. Run the needle back up through the last 2 beads and pull the thread snug (Figure 49). The beads will

Fig.50

now form an upside down V-shape, which will pull together as the work progresses. Put 2 beads on the needle and slide under the thread between the third and fourth beads of the foundation row and then back up through the same two beads. Continue adding 2 beads at a time until you have reached the end of the row (Figure 50). Do not try to tie the last two beads as you have previously done; just start the next row and continue adding beads.

Again, begin with 4 beads on your needle and sew between the second and third bead of the row you just completed (Figure 51).

Fig.51

Work your way down the outside beads until you reach the bottom beads and start the dangles. Due to the height of the tops of this style jewelry, we suggest keeping the dangles shorter than they might normally be. When you reach the top of the piece, add 4 to 6 beads to form a loop for the ear-wire and secure in the normal method, as shown in Figure 52.

Figure 53 illustrates the use of a double stacked row in the center of the "Pumpkin" design.

Fig.52

Fig.53

Beginning The Work

There are two common methods of creating round gourd stitch or so-called peyote beadwork, one which is based on units of two beads and the other which is based on units of three beads. The technique using a two bead unit is best suited for earrings as it is bilaterally symmetric and this is the one we will discuss here.

Creating earrings with gourd stitched tops is best achieved by forming them on a round base, such as a plastic soda straw or a wooden dowel covered with thin buckskin. A clear soda straw can be left in place and will not show, or if the thread is not anchored to the straw in the beginning, it can be removed later after the dangles are added. The di-

ameter of the straw or dowel will determine the size of your earrings and the best size is approximately ¼" in diameter. A 4" to 6" long section makes it easy to work with and this extra length allows you to begin the work a little way up from the end, which will keep the beads from slipping off when first starting the work.

Anchoring your thread at the beginning makes it much easier to start the beadwork. Tie a

Fig.54

double overhand knot about 6" from the end of the thread. If you are using a buckskin covered dowel, knot the end of your thread and run your needle through the buckskin. To use the soda straw, punch an angled hole an inch or two up from the bottom end, running your needle through from the inside so the knot is inside the straw and does not show. See Figure 54.

Next, pick up just enough beads to go completely around the straw (Figure 55) and bring your needle back through the first bead as shown in Figure 56.

Fig.55

This should be an even number of beads and will create the initial row. It is best to select beads that are uniform in shape and they should fit fairly snugly around the soda straw.

Beading **T**he **T**op

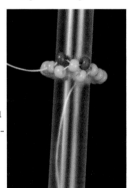

Fig.56

Select another bead, skipping the second bead in the original row, and run your needle through the third bead. This new bead will eventually end up directly above the second bead that you skipped, as shown in Figure 57, but the beads will slide around a bit until the second row is completed. Pick up another bead, and skipping the fourth bead, go through the fifth bead of the original row (Figure 58). Proceed in this manner, adding one bead at a time and skipping over every other bead, until you have added beads all the way around and are back where you started. Run your needle through the next two beads (Figures 59 & 60) and you can add the additional rows of beads in the same manner as described above.

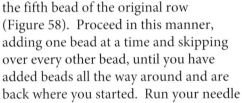

Fig.57

Fig.58

Fig.59   **Fig.60**

Fig.61

Adding The Dangles

When you have completed the beadwork in the length desired for the earring top (Figure 61) add the dangles in any style desired. Most common with this type of earring are the loop dangles as described on page 29 and shown in Figure 66. Variations such as the use of porcupine quills in the fringe also work well or you can use the standard, single strand dangles made of seed beads, (Figure 67) bugle beads or a combination of different types.

Completing The Earring

Next, make a loop of beads at the top for attaching the earwire. This is normally a single strand of 8 to 10 beads as shown in Figure 65. After stringing the beads, attach them directly across to the other side of the earring as shown in Figure 62. Figures 63 and 64 show how to run the needle back through the string of beads to the other side of the earring where it began. Anchor the thread by going back through several beads around the top row and then clip it off.

Fig.62

Fig.63

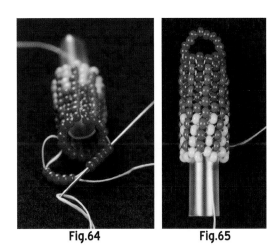

Fig.64   Fig.65

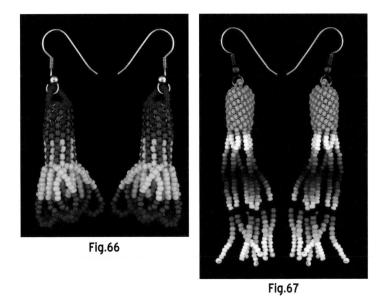

Fig.66

Fig.67

A popular accessory to accompany beaded earrings is the beaded pendant necklace. This is essentially an enlarged version of the earring and is usually made as part of a set consisting of the pendant itself and a pair of matching earrings. The pendant is usually made using the same techniques as previously described for earrings but they are produced in a larger size. Several matching sets are shown in the photos presented here and they illustrate how simple variations in the designs can be quite unique and attractive. Use the graph paper in the design section of the book to plan your designs.

Pendants used for necklaces require a different type of hanger loop than do earrings, as they will be suspended on a beaded chain, cord or leather lace. We recommend making a brick stitch hanger strip for attaching the pendant to the bead chain or other type of necklace, and although other techniques may be used, this style provides a sturdy and most attractive loop.

Necklace Hanger Strips

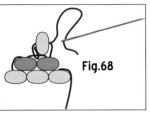

Fig.68

The hanger strip is a loop that is begun in the same way as the loops for earrings but it is made so that the loop opens from side to side rather than front to back as in the case of attaching ear wires. Begin by picking up a single bead and securing it to the thread running across the top two beads of the pendant (Figure

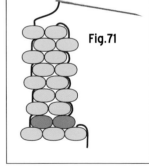

Fig.69

68). Pick up a second bead and run your needle through the thread securing the top row to the second row of beads as shown in Figure 69. Pick up a third bead and begin another row of two beads, then a fourth bead so as to begin forming a row of brick stitch (Figure 70). Continue adding these 2-bead rows (Figure 71) until you have 20 to 24 rows completed.

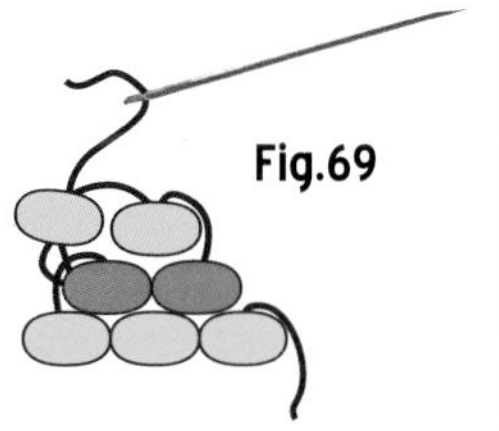

Fold the strip over, lining up the last two beads in the strip directly

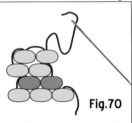

Fig.70

behind the first two beads of the top row of the necklace pendant. This will form a loop that is open from side to side as shown in Figure 72. Secure the loop by running your needle down through the top bead of the pendant and then up through the other bead

Fig.71

at the top of the necklace pendant. Reinforce the loop by running your thread back through all of the beads on one side of the strip, through the top bead again, and then back through all of the beads on the other side of the loop. In this way, there will be double thread through each bead, making the loop much stronger than using only a single thread.

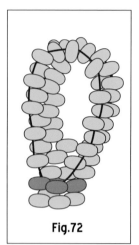

Fig.72

For added variety, these hanging loops can also be made three beads wide instead of just two. The same technique is used but after the first row of two beads is added to the top of the pendant, the next row and each one thereafter will be three beads wide. Figure 73 illustrates a 3-bead wide hanging loop.

You are now ready to run the thread back down through the body of the pendant and begin adding the dangles. Dangles should always be added after the hanger loop at the top so as to reduce the possibility of your working thread becoming tangled with them.

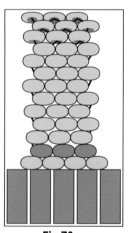

Fig.73

Fig.74

Creating a Beaded Chain

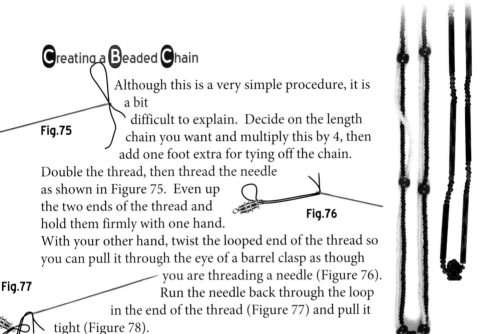

Although this is a very simple procedure, it is a bit difficult to explain. Decide on the length chain you want and multiply this by 4, then add one foot extra for tying off the chain. Double the thread, then thread the needle as shown in Figure 75. Even up the two ends of the thread and hold them firmly with one hand.

Fig.75

Fig.76

With your other hand, twist the looped end of the thread so you can pull it through the eye of a barrel clasp as though you are threading a needle (Figure 76). Run the needle back through the loop in the end of the thread (Figure 77) and pull it tight (Figure 78).

Fig.77

Fig.78

String one seed bead and one bugle bead on the thread and slide them up against the barrel clasp eye. It is always advisable to begin and end a necklace chain with a seed bead because a bugle bead has sharp edges that can cut the thread. Start stringing the beads onto your thread in the desired pattern, keeping the thread from bunching between the beads as you slide each section toward the end of the necklace (Figure 79). A suggested pattern is 1

Fig.79

bugle bead, 5 seed beads, 3 seed beads, 1 center (larger) bead, 3 seed beads, 5 seed beads and 1 bugle bead. Then slide and check the beads. If the thread is pinched and uneven, drop the needle and pinch

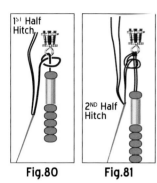

1ˢᵗ Half Hitch

2ⁿᵈ Half Hitch

Fig.80   Fig.81

the thread at the end of the necklace and pull the thread towards the needle. Even up the two ends of the thread and begin working again.

When you reach the desired length of your necklace chain (remembering to end with a seed bead), run the needle through the other eye of the barrel clasp and make a half hitch as shown in Figure 80. This is accomplished by pulling the slack out of the thread and running the needle through the small loop of the thread and pulling it tight. Run the needle through the eye of the barrel clasp once more, repeating the same procedure and again pulling the thread tight (Figure 81). Put a loop in the thread and throw it over the barrel clasp as in Figure 82. Tighten the thread (Figure 83) and run the needle back up through several beads in the chain to hide the end and clip off the extra thread (Figure 84).

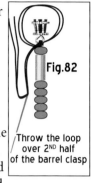

Fig.82

Throw the loop over 2ⁿᵈ half of the barrel clasp

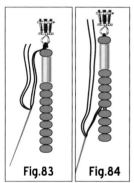

Fig.83   Fig.84

If desired, you may add decorative loops along the necklace chain. This is accomplished with a second pass of the thread, but only through some of the beads of the original necklace.
Instead of tying off the end of the thread as described above, run your needle through the other eye of the barrel clasp, through the end bead and the bugle, then out the first bead in the pattern as illustrated in Figure 85.

Fig.85

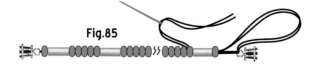

Fig. 86

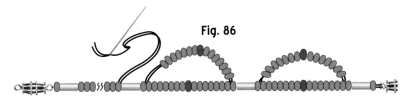

When adding the loops, always subtract one seed bead from each end of the base pattern, and enter one bead before and come out one bead after each bugle. With an initial pattern of 5,3,1,3,5, and a bugle, the second pass will be 4,3,1,3,4 through the first seed bead, the bugle bead and out the next seed bead again (Figure 86). After adding all of the loops and reaching the end (where you started), bring the thread out of the seed bead that is against the eye of the barrel clasp and tie off as described above.

Another nice variation in the necklace chain is the addition of two larger beads in the center of the necklace, on either side of the hanging strip or loop. These can be pony beads, small fire polished AB beads such as 4mm, or similar fancy glass beads of a similar size. These larger beads should be separated by a bugle bead or several seed beads to allow the hanging loop to ride between them.

The necklace chain can also be strung on tiger tail wire and using crimp beads to secure the barrel clasp, which will make a very strong necklace. Tiger tail is a plastic coated, stranded wire that is easy to work with and will not break as easily as thread. See Figure 87, which shows how the crimp beads are used to secure the barrel clasp to the end of the tiger tail.

Tiger Tail Wire

Crimp Bead

Fig.87

The projects on the following pages are laid out so as to allow you to combine several different top sections with different bottoms. There are 7 different patterns for a 15 bead wide top and 5 different patterns for 15 wide sets of dangles. By combining these in different ways, you will be able to choose from 35 different designs. When working with smaller pieces (7 beads wide for example), there are fewer numbers of styles that can be made, which is due to the limited area within which designs can be created. However, by switching just one color, you can have a completely different pattern with which to work. The designs included here are a few of our original geometric styles which will help you get started beading earrings. From here you can go on to create designs of your own using the graphs to experiment with different color combinations and bead types before actually beginning a project. It is much easier to change colors on paper than after you have begun beading.

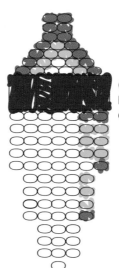

Create your own designs by coloring in the graphs on the following pages.

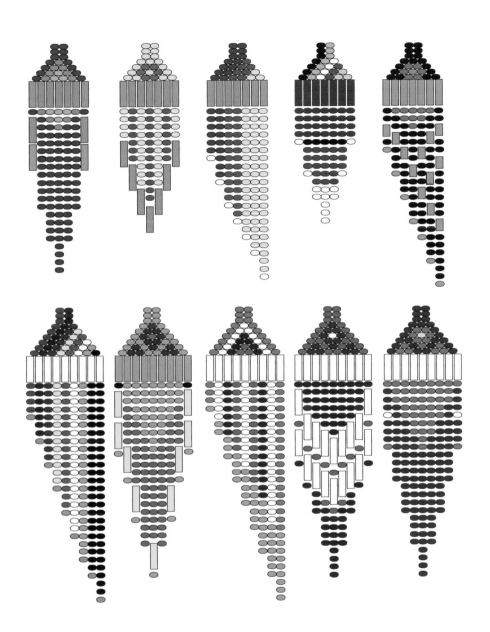

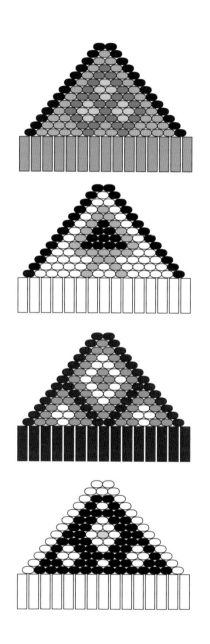

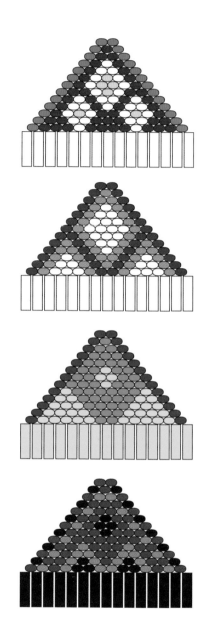

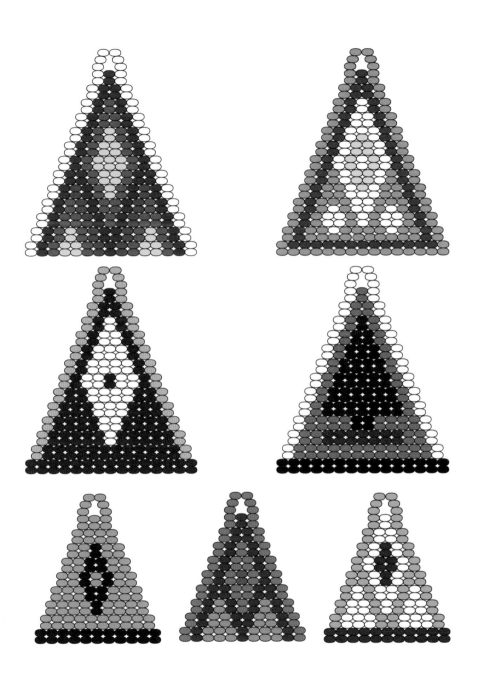

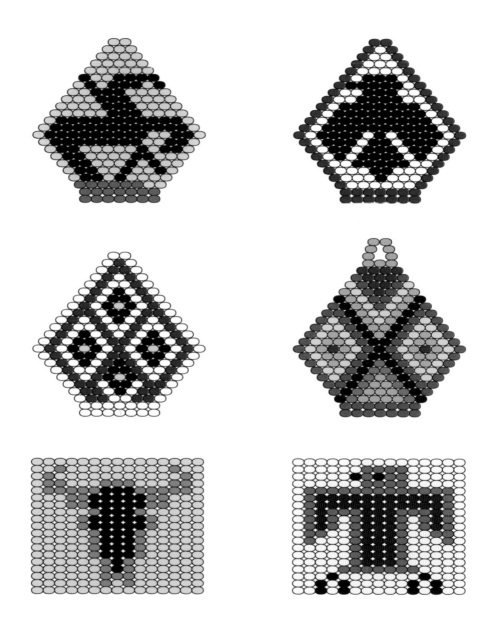

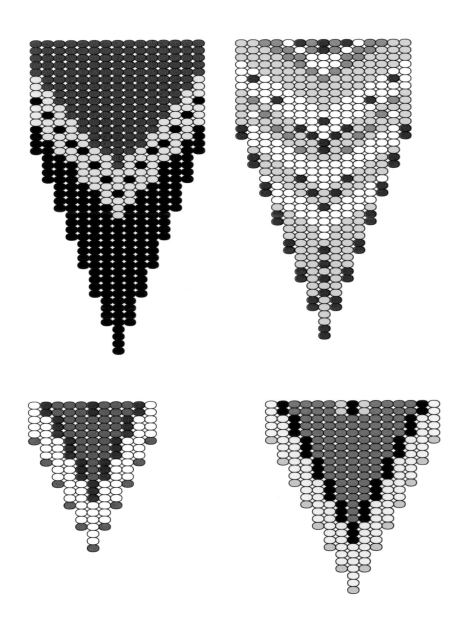

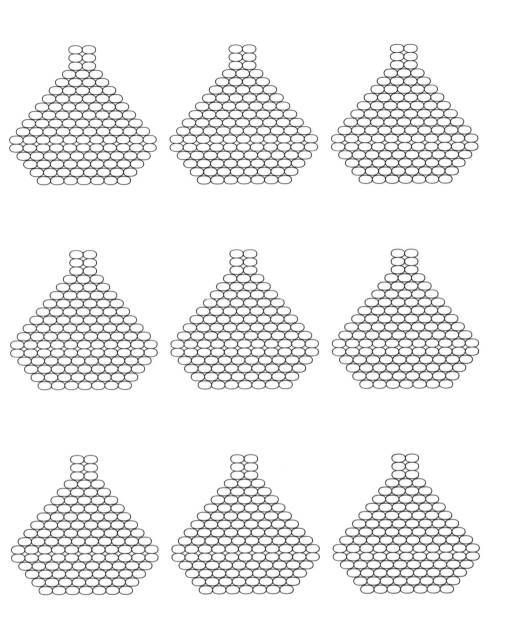

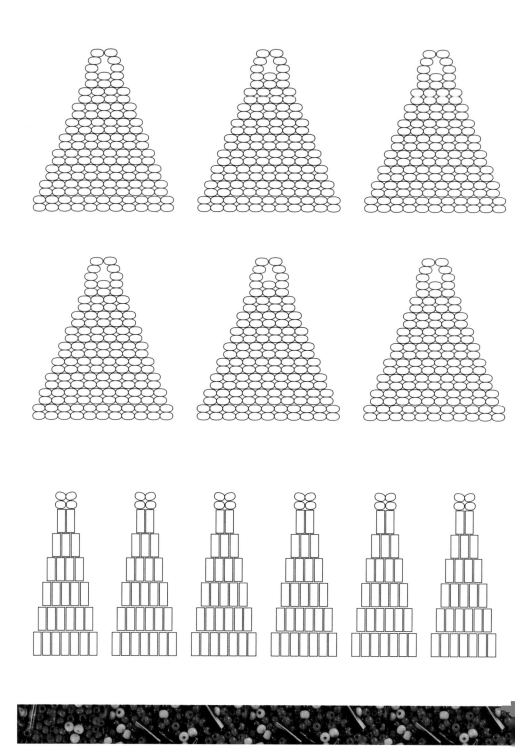

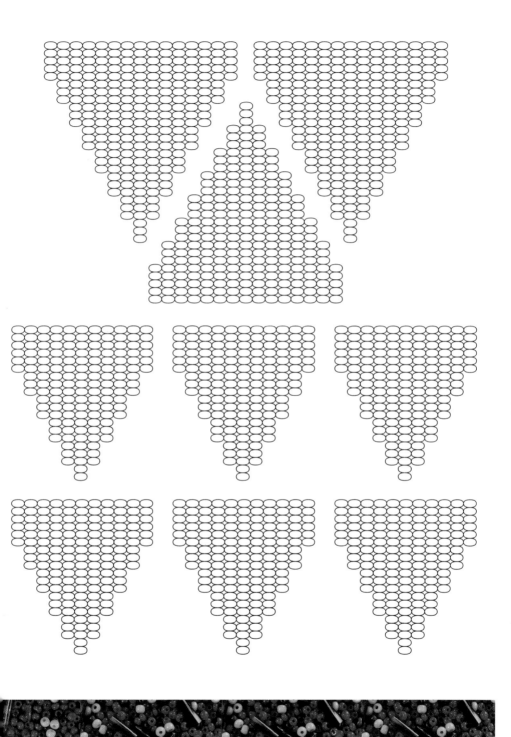

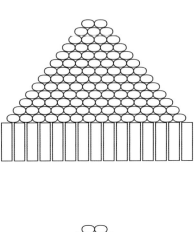

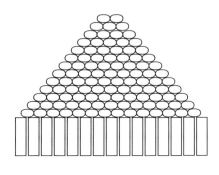

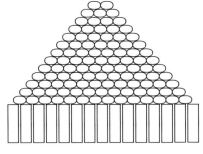

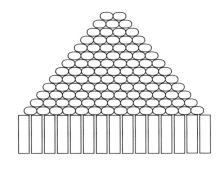

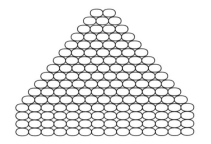

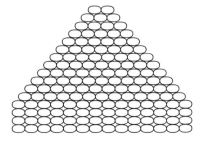

Brick Stitch Graph Paper

Fringe Graph Paper

Example

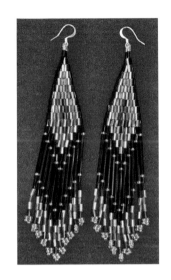

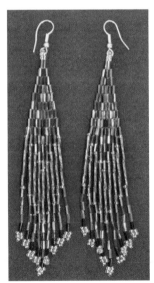

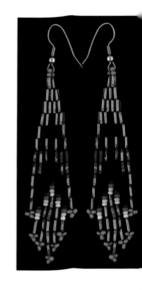

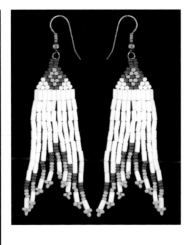

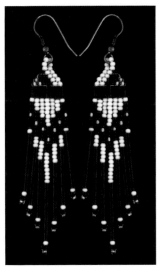

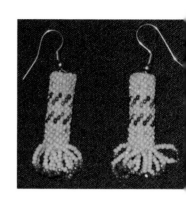

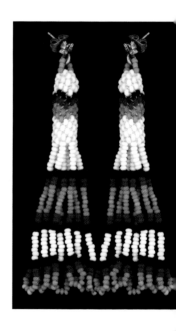